HAL•LEONARD

JAZZ PLAY-ALONG

Book and CD for B♭, E♭, C and Bass Clef Instruments

volume **142**

Charlie Parker Gems

Arranged and Produced by Mark Taylor

BOOK

CD

Photo by William PoPsie Randolph
www.PoPsiePhotos.com

ISBN 978-1-4584-1120-4

HAL•LEONARD®
CORPORATION
7777 W. BLUEMOUND RD. P.O. BOX 13819 MILWAUKEE, WI 53213

Visit Hal Leonard Online at
www.halleonard.com

CHARLIE PARKER GEMS

Volume 142

Arranged and Produced by
Mark Taylor

Featured Players:

Graham Breedlove–Trumpet
John Desalme–Tenor Sax
Tony Nalker–Piano
Jim Roberts–Bass/Guitar
Todd Harrison–Drums

Recorded at Bias Studios, Springfield, Virginia
Bob Dawson, Engineer

HOW TO USE THE CD:

Each song has <u>two</u> tracks:

1) Split Track/Melody

Woodwind, Brass, Keyboard, and **Mallet Players** can use this track as a learning tool for melody style and inflection.

Bass Players can learn and perform with this track – remove the recorded bass track by turning down the volume on the LEFT channel.

Keyboard and **Guitar Players** can learn and perform with this track – remove the recorded piano part by turning down the volume on the RIGHT channel.

2) Full Stereo Track

Soloists or **Groups** can learn and perform with this accompaniment track with the RHYTHM SECTION only.

AH-LEU-CHA

BY CHARLIE PARKER

CD

◆3 : SPLIT TRACK/MELODY

◆4 : FULL STEREO TRACK

BARBADOS

BY CHARLIE PARKER

C VERSION

BIRD OF PARADISE

BY CHARLIE PARKER

C VERSION

CD

BONGO BOP

BY CHARLIE PARKER

C VERSION

MEDIUM SWING

SOLOS (5 CHORUSES)

D.C. AL CODA

CODA

FUNKY BLUES

BY JOHNNY HODGES

CD

11: SPLIT TRACK/MELODY
12: FULL STEREO TRACK

C VERSION

DEWEY SQUARE

BY CHARLIE PARKER

C VERSION

IF I SHOULD LOSE YOU
FROM THE PARAMOUNT PICTURE ROSE OF THE RANCHO

WORDS AND MUSIC BY LEO ROBIN
AND RALPH RAINGER

C VERSION

13

CD

KLACTOUEEDEDSTINE

By Charlie Parker

C VERSION

QUASIMODO

BY CHARLIE PARKER

STAR EYES

CD

19 : SPLIT TRACK/MELODY
20 : FULL STEREO TRACK

WORDS BY DON RAYE
MUSIC BY GENE DEPAUL

C VERSION

AH-LEU-CHA

BY CHARLIE PARKER

Bb VERSION

21

CD

BARBADOS

BY CHARLIE PARKER

Bb VERSION

CD

5 : SPLIT TRACK/MELODY

6 : FULL STEREO TRACK

BIRD OF PARADISE

BY CHARLIE PARKER

Bb VERSION

2ND X ONLY

CD

7 : SPLIT TRACK/MELODY
8 : FULL STEREO TRACK

BONGO BOP

BY CHARLIE PARKER

Bb VERSION

FUNKY BLUES

BY JOHNNY HODGES

CD
🔷 11 : SPLIT TRACK/MELODY
🔷 12 : FULL STEREO TRACK

Bb VERSION

DEWEY SQUARE

BY CHARLIE PARKER

CD
◆ 9 : SPLIT TRACK/MELODY
◆ 10 : FULL STEREO TRACK

KLACTOVEEDSEDSTENE

BY CHARLIE PARKER

QUASIMODO

BY CHARLIE PARKER

CD

17 : SPLIT TRACK/MELODY
18 : FULL STEREO TRACK

Bb VERSION

33

STAR EYES

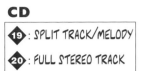

WORDS BY DON RAYE
MUSIC BY GENE DEPAUL

35

CD

AH-LEU-CHA

BY CHARLIE PARKER

Eb VERSION

FINE

37

BARBADOS

BY CHARLIE PARKER

Eb VERSION

MEDIUM LATIN

RHYTHM

ON REPEAT: SWING
ON D.S.: 1ST X SWING, 2ND X LATIN

TO CODA ⊕

SOLOS (6 CHORUSES)
SWING

D.S. AL CODA
TAKE REPEAT

⊕ CODA

CD
5: SPLIT TRACK/MELODY
6: FULL STEREO TRACK

BIRD OF PARADISE

BY CHARLIE PARKER

Eb VERSION

BONGO BOP

BY CHARLIE PARKER

FUNKY BLUES

BY JOHNNY HODGES

Eb VERSION

CD
◆9◆ : SPLIT TRACK/MELODY
◆10◆ : FULL STEREO TRACK

DEWEY SQUARE

BY CHARLIE PARKER

Eb VERSION

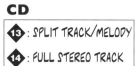

IF I SHOULD LOSE YOU
FROM THE PARAMOUNT PICTURE ROSE OF THE RANCHO

WORDS AND MUSIC BY LEO ROBIN
AND RALPH RAINGER

Eb VERSION

45

RIT.

CD
: SPLIT TRACK/MELODY
: FULL STEREO TRACK

KLACTOVEEDSEDSTENE

BY CHARLIE PARKER

Eb VERSION

CD

QUASIMODO

BY CHARLIE PARKER

Eb VERSION

49

STAR EYES

WORDS BY DON RAYE
MUSIC BY GENE DEPAUL

CD
- 19 : SPLIT TRACK/MELODY
- 20 : FULL STEREO TRACK

Eb VERSION

CD
- 1 : SPLIT TRACK/MELODY
- 2 : FULL STEREO TRACK

AH-LEU-CHA

BY CHARLIE PARKER

𝄢: C VERSION

MEDIUM SWING

SOLO

FINE

CD

❸ : SPLIT TRACK/MELODY
❹ : FULL STEREO TRACK

BARBADOS

BY CHARLIE PARKER

𝄢: C VERSION

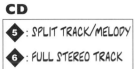

BIRD OF PARADISE

BY CHARLIE PARKER

BONGO BOP

BY CHARLIE PARKER

FUNKY BLUES

BY JOHNNY HODGES

CD

DEWEY SQUARE

BY CHARLIE PARKER

𝄢: C VERSION

60

RIT.

KLACTOVEEDSEDSTENE

By Charlie Parker

CD

17 : SPLIT TRACK/MELODY
18 : FULL STEREO TRACK

QUASIMODO

BY CHARLIE PARKER

𝄢: C VERSION

STAR EYES

WORDS BY DON RAYE
MUSIC BY GENE DePAUL

Presenting the Hal Leonard JAZZ PLAY-ALONG SERIES

For use with all B-flat, E-flat, Bass Clef and C instruments, the Jazz Play-Along® Series is the ultimate learning tool for all jazz musicians. With musician-friendly lead sheets, melody cues, and other split-track choices on the included CD, these first-of-a-kind packages help you master improvisation while playing some of the greatest tunes of all time. FOR STUDY, each tune includes a split track with: melody cue with proper style and inflection • professional rhythm tracks • choruses for soloing • removable bass part • removable piano part. FOR PERFORMANCE, each tune also has: an additional full stereo accompaniment track (no melody) • additional choruses for soloing.

1. DUKE ELLINGTON
00841644...............$16.95

1A. MAIDEN VOYAGE/ALL BLUES
00843158 ....$15.99

2. MILES DAVIS
00841645...............$16.95

3. THE BLUES
00841646...............$16.99

4. JAZZ BALLADS
00841691...............$16.99

5. BEST OF BEBOP
00841689...............$16.95

6. JAZZ CLASSICS WITH EASY CHANGES
00841690...............$16.99

7. ESSENTIAL JAZZ STANDARDS
00843000...............$16.99

8. ANTONIO CARLOS JOBIM AND THE ART OF THE BOSSA NOVA
00843001...............$16.95

9. DIZZY GILLESPIE
00843002...............$16.99

10. DISNEY CLASSICS
00843003...............$16.99

11. RODGERS AND HART FAVORITES
00843004...............$16.99

12. ESSENTIAL JAZZ CLASSICS
00843005...............$16.99

13. JOHN COLTRANE
00843006...............$16.95

14. IRVING BERLIN
00843007...............$15.99

15. RODGERS & HAMMERSTEIN
00843008...............$15.99

16. COLE PORTER
00843009...............$15.95

17. COUNT BASIE
00843010...............$16.95

18. HAROLD ARLEN
00843011...............$15.95

19. COOL JAZZ
00843012...............$15.95

20. CHRISTMAS CAROLS
00843080...............$14.95

21. RODGERS AND HART CLASSICS
00843014...............$14.95

22. WAYNE SHORTER
00843015...............$16.95

23. LATIN JAZZ
00843016...............$16.95

24. EARLY JAZZ STANDARDS
00843017...............$14.95

25. CHRISTMAS JAZZ
00843018...............$16.95

26. CHARLIE PARKER
00843019...............$16.95

27. GREAT JAZZ STANDARDS
00843020...............$16.99

28. BIG BAND ERA
00843021...............$15.99

29. LENNON AND MCCARTNEY
00843022...............$16.95

30. BLUES' BEST
00843023...............$15.99

31. JAZZ IN THREE
00843024...............$15.99

32. BEST OF SWING
00843025...............$15.99

33. SONNY ROLLINS
00843029...............$15.95

34. ALL TIME STANDARDS
00843030...............$15.99

35. BLUESY JAZZ
00843031...............$16.99

36. HORACE SILVER
00843032...............$16.99

37. BILL EVANS
00843033...............$16.95

38. YULETIDE JAZZ
00843034...............$16.95

39. "ALL THE THINGS YOU ARE" & MORE JEROME KERN SONGS
00843035...............$15.99

40. BOSSA NOVA
00843036...............$15.99

41. CLASSIC DUKE ELLINGTON
00843037...............$16.99

42. GERRY MULLIGAN FAVORITES
00843038...............$16.99

43. GERRY MULLIGAN CLASSICS
00843039...............$16.95

44. OLIVER NELSON
00843040...............$16.95

45. JAZZ AT THE MOVIES
00843041...............$15.99

46. BROADWAY JAZZ STANDARDS
00843042...............$15.99

47. CLASSIC JAZZ BALLADS
00843043...............$15.99

48. BEBOP CLASSICS
00843044...............$16.99

49. MILES DAVIS STANDARDS
00843045...............$16.95

50. GREAT JAZZ CLASSICS
00843046...............$15.99

51. UP-TEMPO JAZZ
00843047...............$15.99

52. STEVIE WONDER
00843048...............$16.99

53. RHYTHM CHANGES
00843049...............$15.99

54. "MOONLIGHT IN VERMONT" AND OTHER GREAT STANDARDS
00843050...............$15.99

55. BENNY GOLSON
00843052...............$15.95

56. "GEORGIA ON MY MIND" & OTHER SONGS BY HOAGY CARMICHAEL
00843056 ....$15.99

57. VINCE GUARALDI
00843057...............$16.99

58. MORE LENNON AND MCCARTNEY
00843059...............$15.99

59. SOUL JAZZ
00843060...............$15.99

60. DEXTER GORDON
00843061 ....$15.95

61. MONGO SANTAMARIA
00843062...............$15.95

62. JAZZ-ROCK FUSION
00843063...............$16.99

63. CLASSICAL JAZZ 00843064 ....$14.95	**92. LEONARD BERNSTEIN** 00450134 ....$15.99	**120. J.S. BACH** 00843169 ....$15.99
64. TV TUNES 00843065 ....$14.95	**93. DISNEY FAVORITES** 00843142 ....$14.99	**121. DJANGO REINHARDT** 00843170 ....$15.99
65. SMOOTH JAZZ 00843066 ....$16.99	**94. RAY** 00843143 ....$14.99	**122. PAUL SIMON** 00843182 ....$16.99
66. A CHARLIE BROWN CHRISTMAS 00843067 ....$16.99	**95. JAZZ AT THE LOUNGE** 00843144 ....V$14.99	**123. BACHARACH & DAVID** 00843185 ....$15.99
67. CHICK COREA 00843068 ....$15.95	**96. LATIN JAZZ STANDARDS** 00843145 ....$14.99	**124. JAZZ-ROCK HORN HITS** 00843186 ....$15.99
68. CHARLES MINGUS 00843069 ....$16.95	**97. MAYBE I'M AMAZED** * 00843148 ....$15.99	**126. COUNT BASIE CLASSICS** 00843157 ....$15.99
69. CLASSIC JAZZ 00843071 ....$15.99	**98. DAVE FRISHBERG** 00843149 ....$15.99	**127. CHUCK MANGIONE** 00843188 ....$15.99
70. THE DOORS 00843072 ....$14.95	**99. SWINGING STANDARDS** 00843150 ....$14.99	**132. STAN GETZ ESSENTIALS** 00843193 ....$15.99
71. COLE PORTER CLASSICS 00843073 ....$14.95	**100. LOUIS ARMSTRONG** 00740423 ....$15.99	**133. STAN GETZ FAVORITES** 00843194 ....$15.99
72. CLASSIC JAZZ BALLADS 00843074 ....$15.99	**101. BUD POWELL** 00843152 ....$14.99	**134. NURSERY RHYMES** * 00843196 ....$17.99
73. JAZZ/BLUES 00843075 ....$14.95	**102. JAZZ POP** 00843153 ....$14.99	**135. JEFF BECK** 00843197 ....$15.99
74. BEST JAZZ CLASSICS 00843076 ....$15.99	**103. ON GREEN DOLPHIN STREET & OTHER JAZZ CLASSICS** 00843154 ....$14.99	**136. NAT ADDERLEY** 00843198 ....$15.99
75. PAUL DESMOND 00843077 ....$14.95	**104. ELTON JOHN** 00843155 ....$14.99	**137. WES MONTGOMERY** 00843199 ....$15.99
76. BROADWAY JAZZ BALLADS 00843078 ....$15.99	**105. SOULFUL JAZZ** 00843151 ....$15.99	**138. FREDDIE HUBBARD** 00843200 ....$15.99
77. JAZZ ON BROADWAY 00843079 ....$15.99	**106. SLO' JAZZ** 00843117 ....$14.99	**139. JULIAN "CANNONBALL" ADDERLEY** 00843201 ....$15.99
78. STEELY DAN 00843070 ....$14.99	**107. MOTOWN CLASSICS** 00843116 ....$14.99	**141. BILL EVANS STANDARDS** 00843156 ....$15.99
79. MILES DAVIS CLASSICS 00843081 ....$15.99	**108. JAZZ WALTZ** 00843159 ....$15.99	**150. JAZZ IMPROV BASICS** 00843195 ....$19.99
80. JIMI HENDRIX 00843083 ....$15.99	**109. OSCAR PETERSON** 00843160 ....$16.99	**151. MODERN JAZZ QUARTET CLASSICS** 00843209 ....$15.99
81. FRANK SINATRA – CLASSICS 00843084 ....$15.99	**110. JUST STANDARDS** 00843161 ....$15.99	**157. HYMNS** 00843217 ....$15.99
82. FRANK SINATRA – STANDARDS 00843085 ....$15.99	**111. COOL CHRISTMAS** 00843162 ....$15.99	**162. BIG CHRISTMAS COLLECTION** 00843221 ....$24.99
83. ANDREW LLOYD WEBBER 00843104 ....$14.95	**112. PAQUITO D'RIVERA – LATIN JAZZ** * 48020662 ....$16.99	
84. BOSSA NOVA CLASSICS 00843105 ....$14.95	**113. PAQUITO D'RIVERA – BRAZILIAN JAZZ** * 48020663 ....$19.99	
85. MOTOWN HITS 00843109 ....$14.95	**114. MODERN JAZZ QUARTET FAVORITES** 00843163 ....$15.99	
86. BENNY GOODMAN 00843110 ....$14.95	**115. THE SOUND OF MUSIC** 00843164 ....$15.99	
87. DIXIELAND 00843111 ....$14.95	**116. JACO PASTORIUS** 00843165 ....$15.99	**HAL•LEONARD®** CORPORATION
88. DUKE ELLINGTON FAVORITES 00843112 ....$14.95	**117. ANTONIO CARLOS JOBIM – MORE HITS** 00843166 ....$15.99	7777 W. BLUEMOUND RD. P.O. BOX 13819 MILWAUKEE, WISCONSIN 53213
89. IRVING BERLIN FAVORITES 00843113 ....$14.95	**118. BIG JAZZ STANDARDS COLLECTION** 00843167 ....$27.50	For complete songlists and more, visit Hal Leonard online at
90. THELONIOUS MONK CLASSICS 00841262 ....$16.99	**119. JELLY ROLL MORTON** 00843168 ....$15.99	**www.halleonard.com**
91.THELONIOUS MONK FAVORITES 00841263 ....$16.99		

* These CDs do not include split tracks.

Jazz Instruction & Improvisation
Books for All Instruments from Hal Leonard

AN APPROACH TO JAZZ IMPROVISATION
by Dave Pozzi
Musicians Institute Press

INCLUDES TAB

Explore the styles of Charlie Parker, Sonny Rollins, Bud Powell and others with this comprehensive guide to jazz improvisation. Covers: scale choices • chord analysis • phrasing • melodies • harmonic progressions • more.
00695135 Book/CD Pack $17.95

BUILDING A JAZZ VOCABULARY
By Mike Steinel

A valuable resource for learning the basics of jazz from Mike Steinel of the University of North Texas. It covers: the basics of jazz • how to build effective solos • a comprehensive practice routine • and a jazz vocabulary of the masters.
00849911 ....$19.95

THE CYCLE OF FIFTHS
by Emile and Laura De Cosmo

This essential instruction book provides more than 450 exercises, including hundreds of melodic and rhythmic ideas. The book is designed to help improvisors master the cycle of fifths, one of the primary progressions in music. Guaranteed to refine technique, enhance improvisational fluency, and improve sight-reading!
00311114 ....$16.99

THE DIATONIC CYCLE
by Emile and Laura De Cosmo

Renowned jazz educators Emile and Laura De Cosmo provide more than 300 exercises to help improvisors tackle one of music's most common progressions: the diatonic cycle. This book is guaranteed to refine technique, enhance improvisational fluency, and improve sight-reading!
00311115 ....$16.95

EAR TRAINING
by Keith Wyatt,
Carl Schroeder and Joe Elliott
Musicians Institute Press

Covers: basic pitch matching • singing major and minor scales • identifying intervals • transcribing melodies and rhythm • identifying chords and progressions • seventh chords and the blues • modal interchange, chromaticism, modulation • and more.
00695198 Book/2-CD Pack....................................$24.95

EXERCISES AND ETUDES FOR THE JAZZ INSTRUMENTALIST
by J.J. Johnson

Designed as study material and playable by any instrument, these pieces run the gamut of the jazz experience, featuring common and uncommon time signatures and keys, and styles from ballads to funk. They are progressively graded so that both beginners and professionals will be challenged by the demands of this wonderful music.
00842018 Bass Clef Edition...................................$16.95
00842042 Treble Clef Edition $16.95

JAZZOLOGY
THE ENCYCLOPEDIA OF JAZZ THEORY FOR ALL MUSICIANS
by Robert Rawlins and Nor Eddine Bahha

This comprehensive resource covers a variety of jazz topics, for beginners and pros of any instrument. The book serves as an encyclopedia for reference, a thorough methodology for the student, and a workbook for the classroom.
00311167 ....$19.99

JAZZ JAM SESSION
15 TRACKS INCLUDING RHYTHM CHANGES, BLUES, BOSSA, BALLADS & MORE
by Ed Friedland

Bring your local jazz jam session home! These essential jazz rhythm grooves feature a professional rhythm section and are perfect for guitar, harmonica, keyboard, saxophone and trumpet players to hone their soloing skills. The feels, tempos and keys have been varied to broaden your jazz experience. Styles include: ballads, bebop, blues, bossa nova, cool jazz, and more, with improv guidelines for each track.
00311827 Book/CD Pack $19.99

JAZZ THEORY RESOURCES
by Bert Ligon
Houston Publishing, Inc.

This is a jazz theory text in two volumes. **Volume 1 includes:** review of basic theory • rhythm in jazz performance • triadic generalization • diatonic harmonic progressions and analysis • substitutions and turnarounds • and more. **Volume 2 includes:** modes and modal frameworks • quartal harmony • extended tertian structures and triadic superimposition • pentatonic applications • coloring "outside" the lines and beyond • and more.
00030458 Volume 1..$39.95
00030459 Volume 2..$29.95

JOY OF IMPROV
by Dave Frank and John Amaral

This book/CD course on improvisation for all instruments and all styles will help players develop monster musical skills! **Book One** imparts a solid basis in technique, rhythm, chord theory, ear training and improv concepts. **Book Two** explores more advanced chord voicings, chord arranging techniques and more challenging blues and melodic lines. The CD can be used as a listening and play-along tool.
00220005 Book 1 – Book/CD Pack $27.99
00220006 Book 2 – Book/CD Pack $24.95

THE PATH TO JAZZ IMPROVISATION
by Emile and Laura De Cosmo

This fascinating jazz instruction book offers an innovative, scholarly approach to the art of improvisation. It includes in-depth analysis and lessons about: cycle of fifths • diatonic cycle • overtone series • pentatonic scale • harmonic and melodic minor scale • polytonal order of keys • blues and bebop scales • modes • and more.
00310904 ....$14.95

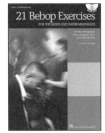

THE SOURCE
THE DICTIONARY OF CONTEMPORARY AND TRADITIONAL SCALES
by Steve Barta

This book serves as an informative guide for people who are looking for good, solid information regarding scales, chords, and how they work together. It provides right and left hand fingerings for scales, chords, and complete inversions. Includes over 20 different scales, each written in all 12 keys.
00240885 ....$17.99

21 BEBOP EXERCISES
by Steve Rawlins

This book/CD pack is both a warm-up collection and a manual for bebop phrasing. Its tasty and sophisticated exercises will help you develop your proficiency with jazz interpretation. It concentrates on practice in all twelve keys – moving higher by half-step – to help develop dexterity and range. The companion CD includes all of the exercises in 12 keys.
00315341 Book/CD Pack $17.95

FOR MORE INFORMATION, SEE YOUR LOCAL MUSIC DEALER, OR WRITE TO:

HAL•LEONARD® CORPORATION
7777 W. BLUEMOUND RD. P.O. BOX 13819 MILWAUKEE, WI 53213

Prices, contents & availability subject to change without notice.

Visit Hal Leonard online at
www.halleonard.com

0911

ARTIST TRANSCRIPTIONS®

Artist Transcriptions are authentic, note-for-note transcriptions of today's hottest artists in jazz, pop and rock. These outstanding, accurate arrangements are in an easy-to-read format which includes all essential lines. Artist Transcriptions can be used to perform, sequence or for reference.

CLARINET

| 00672423 | Buddy De Franco Collection | $19.95 |

FLUTE

00672379	Eric Dolphy Collection	$19.95
00672372	James Moody Collection – Sax and Flute	$19.95
00660108	James Newton – Improvising Flute	$14.95

GUITAR & BASS

00660113	The Guitar Style of George Benson	$14.95
00699072	Guitar Book of Pierre Bensusan	$29.95
00672331	Ron Carter – Acoustic Bass	$16.95
00672307	Stanley Clarke Collection	$19.95
00660115	Al Di Meola – Friday Night in San Francisco	$14.95
00604043	Al Di Meola – Music, Words, Pictures	$14.95
00673245	Jazz Style of Tal Farlow	$19.95
00672359	Bela Fleck and the Flecktones	$18.95
00699389	Jim Hall – Jazz Guitar Environments	$19.95
00699306	Jim Hall – Exploring Jazz Guitar	$19.95
00604049	Allan Holdsworth – Reaching for the Uncommon Chord	$14.95
00699215	Leo Kottke – Eight Songs	$14.95
00675536	Wes Montgomery – Guitar Transcriptions	$17.95
00672353	Joe Pass Collection	$18.95
00673216	John Patitucci	$16.95
00027083	Django Reinhardt Anthology	$14.95
00026711	Genius of Django Reinhardt	$10.95
00672374	Johnny Smith Guitar Solos	$16.95
00672320	Mark Whitfield	$19.95

PIANO & KEYBOARD

00672338	Monty Alexander Collection	$19.95
00672487	Monty Alexander Plays Standards	$19.95
00672318	Kenny Barron Collection	$22.95
00672520	Count Basie Collection	$19.95
00672364	Warren Bernhardt Collection	$19.95
00672439	Cyrus Chestnut Collection	$19.95
00673242	Billy Childs Collection	$19.95
00672300	Chick Corea – Paint the World	$12.95
00672537	Bill Evans at Town Hall	$16.95
00672425	Bill Evans – Piano Interpretations	$19.95
00672365	Bill Evans – Piano Standards	$19.95
00672510	Bill Evans Trio – Vol. 1: 1959-1961	$24.95
00672511	Bill Evans Trio – Vol. 2: 1962-1965	$24.95
00672512	Bill Evans Trio – Vol. 3: 1968-1974	$24.95
00672513	Bill Evans Trio – Vol. 4: 1979-1980	$24.95
00672381	Tommy Flanagan Collection	$24.99
00672492	Benny Goodman Collection	$16.95
00672486	Vince Guaraldi Collection	$19.95
00672419	Herbie Hancock Collection	$19.95
00672438	Hampton Hawes	$19.95

00672322	Ahmad Jamal Collection	$22.95
00672564	Best of Jeff Lorber	$17.99
00672476	Brad Mehldau Collection	$19.99
00672388	Best of Thelonious Monk	$19.95
00672389	Thelonious Monk Collection	$19.95
00672390	Thelonious Monk Plays Jazz Standards – Volume 1	$19.95
00672391	Thelonious Monk Plays Jazz Standards – Volume 2	$19.95
00672433	Jelly Roll Morton – The Piano Rolls	$12.95
00672553	Charlie Parker for Piano	$19.95
00672542	Oscar Peterson – Jazz Piano Solos	$16.95
00672544	Oscar Peterson – Originals	$9.95
00672532	Oscar Peterson – Plays Broadway	$19.95
00672531	Oscar Peterson – Plays Duke Ellington	$19.95
00672563	Oscar Peterson – A Royal Wedding Suite	$19.99
00672533	Oscar Peterson – Trios	$24.95
00672543	Oscar Peterson Trio – Canadiana Suite	$9.95
00672534	Very Best of Oscar Peterson	$22.95
00672371	Bud Powell Classics	$19.95
00672376	Bud Powell Collection	$19.95
00672437	André Previn Collection	$19.95
00672507	Gonzalo Rubalcaba Collection	$19.95
00672303	Horace Silver Collection	$19.95
00672316	Art Tatum Collection	$22.95
00672355	Art Tatum Solo Book	$19.95
00672357	Billy Taylor Collection	$24.95
00673215	McCoy Tyner	$16.95
00672321	Cedar Walton Collection	$19.95
00672519	Kenny Werner Collection	$19.95
00672434	Teddy Wilson Collection	$19.95

SAXOPHONE

00672566	The Mindi Abair Collection	$14.99
00673244	Julian "Cannonball" Adderley Collection	$19.95
00673237	Michael Brecker	$19.95
00672429	Michael Brecker Collection	$19.95
00672315	Benny Carter Plays Standards	$22.95
00672314	Benny Carter Collection	$22.95
00672394	James Carter Collection	$19.95
00672349	John Coltrane Plays Giant Steps	$19.95
00672529	John Coltrane – Giant Steps	$14.95
00672494	John Coltrane – A Love Supreme	$14.95
00672493	John Coltrane Plays "Coltrane Changes"	$19.95
00672453	John Coltrane Plays Standards	$19.95
00673233	John Coltrane Solos	$22.95
00672328	Paul Desmond Collection	$19.95
00672379	Eric Dolphy Collection	$19.95
00672530	Kenny Garrett Collection	$19.95
00699375	Stan Getz	$19.95
00672377	Stan Getz – Bossa Novas	$19.95
00672375	Stan Getz – Standards	$18.95
00673254	Great Tenor Sax Solos	$18.95

00672523	Coleman Hawkins Collection	$19.95
00673252	Joe Henderson – Selections from "Lush Life" & "So Near So Far"	$19.95
00672330	Best of Joe Henderson	$22.95
00673239	Best of Kenny G	$19.95
00673229	Kenny G – Breathless	$19.95
00672462	Kenny G – Classics in the Key of G	$19.95
00672485	Kenny G – Faith: A Holiday Album	$14.95
00672373	Kenny G – The Moment	$19.95
00672326	Joe Lovano Collection	$19.95
00672498	Jackie McLean Collection	$19.95
00672372	James Moody Collection – Sax and Flute	$19.95
00672416	Frank Morgan Collection	$19.95
00672539	Gerry Mulligan Collection	$19.95
00672352	Charlie Parker Collection	$19.95
00672561	Best of Sonny Rollins	$19.95
00672444	Sonny Rollins Collection	$19.95
00675000	David Sanborn Collection	$17.95
00672528	Bud Shank Collection	$19.95
00672491	New Best of Wayne Shorter	$19.95
00672550	The Sonny Stitt Collection	$19.95
00672350	Tenor Saxophone Standards	$18.95
00672567	The Best of Kim Waters	$17.99
00672524	Lester Young Collection	$19.95

TROMBONE

| 00672332 | J.J. Johnson Collection | $19.95 |
| 00672489 | Steve Turré Collection | $19.95 |

TRUMPET

00672557	Herb Alpert Collection	$14.99
00672480	Louis Armstrong Collection	$17.95
00672481	Louis Armstrong Plays Standards	$17.95
00672435	Chet Baker Collection	$19.95
00672556	Best of Chris Botti	$19.95
00672448	Miles Davis – Originals, Vol. 1	$19.95
00672451	Miles Davis – Originals, Vol. 2	$19.95
00672450	Miles Davis – Standards, Vol. 1	$19.95
00672449	Miles Davis – Standards, Vol. 2	$19.95
00672479	Dizzy Gillespie Collection	$19.95
00673214	Freddie Hubbard	$14.95
00672382	Tom Harrell – Jazz Trumpet	$19.95
00672363	Jazz Trumpet Solos	$9.95
00672506	Chuck Mangione Collection	$19.95
00672525	Arturo Sandoval – Trumpet Evolution	$19.95

FOR MORE INFORMATION, SEE YOUR LOCAL MUSIC DEALER, OR WRITE TO:

HAL•LEONARD® CORPORATION

7777 W. BLUEMOUND RD. P.O. BOX 13819 MILWAUKEE, WI 53213

Visit our web site for a complete listing of our titles with songlists at
www.halleonard.com

Prices and availability subject to change without notice.

0310

The Best-Selling Jazz Book of All Time Is Now Legal!

The Real Books are the most popular jazz books of all time. Since the 1970s, musicians have trusted these volumes to get them through every gig, night after night. The problem is that the books were illegally produced and distributed, without any regard to copyright law, or royalties paid to the composers who created these musical masterpieces.

Hal Leonard is very proud to present the first legitimate and legal editions of these books ever produced. You won't even notice the difference, other than all the notorious errors being fixed: the covers and typeface look the same, the song lists are nearly identical, and the price for our edition is even cheaper than the originals!

Every conscientious musician will appreciate that these books are now produced accurately and ethically, benefitting the songwriters that we owe for some of the greatest tunes of all time!

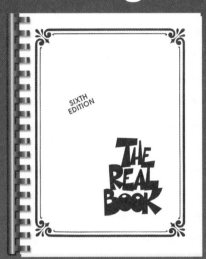

VOLUME 1
Includes: Autumn Leaves • Body and Soul • Don't Get Around Much Anymore • Falling in Love with Love • Have You Met Miss Jones? • Lullaby of Birdland • Misty • Satin Doll • Stella by Starlight • and hundreds more!

00240221	C Edition	$29.99
00240224	B♭ Edition	$29.95
00240225	E♭ Edition	$29.99
00240226	Bass Clef Edition	$29.95
00240292	C Edition 6 x 9	$27.95
00451087	C Edition on CD-ROM	$25.00

VOLUME 2
Includes: Avalon • Birdland • Come Rain or Come Shine • Fever • Georgia on My Mind • It Might as Well Be Spring • Moonglow • The Nearness of You • On the Sunny Side of the Street • Route 66 • Sentimental Journey • Smoke Gets in Your Eyes • Tangerine • Yardbird Suite • and more!

00240222	C Edition	$29.99
00240227	B♭ Edition	$29.95
00240228	E♭ Edition	$29.95
00240229	Bass Clef Edition	$29.95
00240293	C Edition 6 x 9	$27.95

VOLUME 3
Includes: Ain't Misbehavin' • Cheek to Cheek • The Lady Is a Tramp • A Nightingale Sang in Berkeley Square • On a Clear Day • Stormy Weather • The Very Thought of You • and more!

00240233	C Edition	$29.99
00240284	B♭ Edition	$29.95
00240285	E♭ Edition	$29.95
00240286	Bass Clef Edition	$29.95

VOLUME 4
Includes: The Best Is Yet to Come • A Foggy Day (In London Town) • I Got Rhythm • Kansas City • Night and Day • Ol' Man River • Smile • Them There Eyes • and more!

00240296	C Edition	$29.99

Play-along CDs to some of the most popular songs featured in the world famous *Real Books* are available. Each volume features selections sorted alphabetically from the 6th edition, each in 3-CD sets.

The Real Book Play-Along – Volume 1
00240302	A-D	$24.99
00240303	E-J	$24.95
00240304	L-R	$24.95
00240305	S-Z	$24.99

The Real Book Play-Along – Volume 2
00240351	A-D	$24.99
00240352	E-I	$24.99
00240353	J-R	$24.99
00240354	S-Z	$24.99

Also available:
00240264	The Real Blues Book	$34.99
00240306	The Real Christmas Book	$25.00
00240137	Miles Davis Real Book	$19.95
00240235	The Duke Ellington Real Book	$19.99
00240331	The Bud Powell Real Book	$19.99
00240313	The Real Rock Book	$29.99
00240359	The Real Tab Book – Vol. 1	$32.50
00310910	The Real Bluegrass Book	$29.99
00240355	The Real Dixieland Book	$29.99
00240317	The Real Worship Book	$29.99

THE REAL VOCAL BOOK
00240230	Volume 1 High Voice	$29.95
00240307	Volume 1 Low Voice	$29.99
00240231	Volume 2 High Voice	$29.95
00240308	Volume 2 Low Voice	$29.95

THE REAL BOOK – STAFF PAPER
00240327		$9.95

Complete song lists online at www.halleonard.com
Prices and availability subject to change without notice.

FOR MORE INFORMATION, SEE YOUR LOCAL MUSIC DEALER, OR WRITE TO:

HAL•LEONARD® CORPORATION

7777 W. BLUEMOUND RD. P.O. BOX 13819 MILWAUKEE, WI 53213

0111